Super Cute Things to Draw
Everything Cats

Lulu Mayo

Walter Foster

Quarto.com

This library edition published in 2024 by Walter Foster Publishing, an imprint of The Quarto Group.

100 Cummings Center, Suite 265-D, Beverly, MA 01915, USA.
T (978) 282-9590 F (978) 283-2742

Distributed in the United States and Canada
by Lerner Publisher Services
241 First Avenue North
Minneapolis, MN 55401 U.S.A.
www.lernerbooks.com

First Library Edition

Library of Congress Cataloging-in-Publication Data

Names: Mayo, Lulu, author, illustrator.
Title: Super cute things to draw : everything cats / Lulu Mayo.
Description: Lerner. | Beverly, MA : Walter Foster, [2024] | Audience: Ages 8-12 | Audience: Grades 4-6 | Summary: "Everything Cats includes step-by-step drawing projects for cat lovers of all ages-with easy-to-follow lessons, whimsical doodles, and aww-inspiring cat mash-ups"-- Provided by publisher.
Identifiers: LCCN 2024005071 | ISBN 9780760391198 (hardcover)
Subjects: LCSH: Cats in art--Juvenile literature. | Drawing--Technique--Juvenile literature.
Classification: LCC NC783.8.C36 M39 2024 | DDC 743.6/975--dc23/eng/20240307
LC record available at https://lccn.loc.gov/2024005071

Printed in USA
10 9 8 7 6 5 4 3 2 1

Table of Contents

INTRODUCTION

Welcome to the world of almost unbearable cat cuteness!

Created for cat lovers, doodle enthusiasts, and artists of all ages and skill levels, ***Super Cute Things to Draw*** is where creativity and fun intersect with fluffy felines in delightful cat-themed drawing projects.

If you are crazy about cats or looking for new ways to get inspired to draw, you are in the right place. This adorable book is designed to provide you an escape to a relaxing world of quirkiness and creativity.

I like to bring energy and happiness to my work. My hope is that when you pick up your pencil and follow along, you will experience those same feelings.

So let your imagination run wild and lose yourself in doodling!

~Lulu Mayo

TOOLS & MATERIALS

Here are some basic tools and materials to get you started with the projects in this book.

Colored Pencils – Colored pencils are a convenient and easy tool for applying color. Professional-grade colored pencils have a waxy, soft lead that is excellent for shading and building up layers of color.

Pencils – Graphite drawing pencils are designated by hardness and softness. H pencils are hard and make lighter marks; B pencils are soft and make darker marks. Pencils range from very soft (9B) to very hard (9H). You can also use a plain old No. 2 pencil if that's what works for you!

Sketchpad – Sketchpads come in many sizes and are great for practicing and doodling.

Crayons – Who doesn't love to color with crayon? Crayons are perfect for outlining and coloring in large areas.

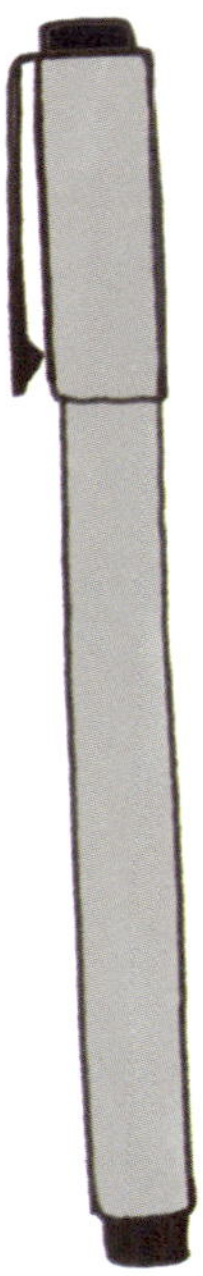

Pigment-Ink Pens – Technical pens are great for adding small details.

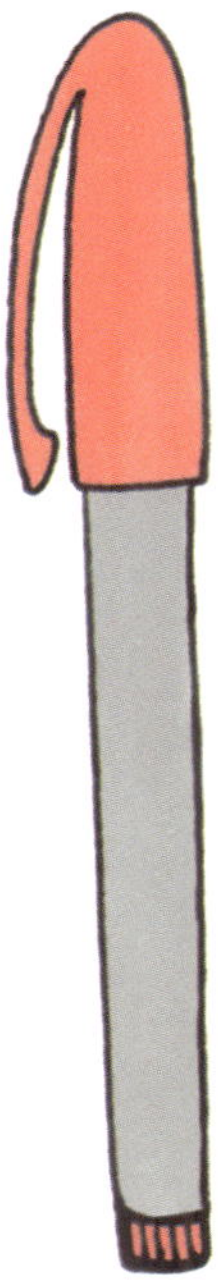

Art Markers – Art markers create bold, vibrant bands of color. They are great for laying down large areas of even color, as well as for shading and creating patterns.

Eraser – Plastic or vinyl erasers are a staple in drawing. They remove graphite without messing up the paper and are best for erasing hard pencil marks and large areas.

GETTING STARTED

All drawings start with a line—and simple lines can be very expressive. You can use them to show emotion, personality, or movement. Here are some examples:

ADDING COLOR

There are many ways to use your coloring tools to create a variety of strokes and unique effects.

Techniques

HATCHING

Hatching is a series of parallel lines going in one direction, either vertically or horizontally.

The closer the hatching lines are to each other, the denser and darker the color.

CROSSHATCHING

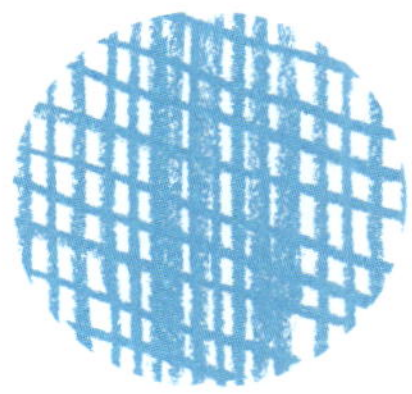

Crosshatching involves layering one set of hatched lines over another, but in a different direction.

SCUMBLING

Create this effect by scribbling your pencil randomly to create a mass of color.

STIPPLING

Apply small dots of color close together to create dense color and pattern.

BLENDING

To blend one color into another, lighten the pressure of your pencil and overlap the strokes where the colors meet.

LAYERING

Mix colors of your choice by layering them lightly. In this example, look how layering yellow over dark green results in a lighter green.

GRADATING

Gradation is a lightening or darkening of a color or the blending of colors. To create a gradation, stroke side to side with heavy pressure and lighten the pressure as you move to show a clear color transition.

THE COLOR WHEEL

Color can help bring your drawings to life! A color wheel is useful for understanding relationships between colors. Use the color wheel when you want to find the purrfect color schemes for your drawings.

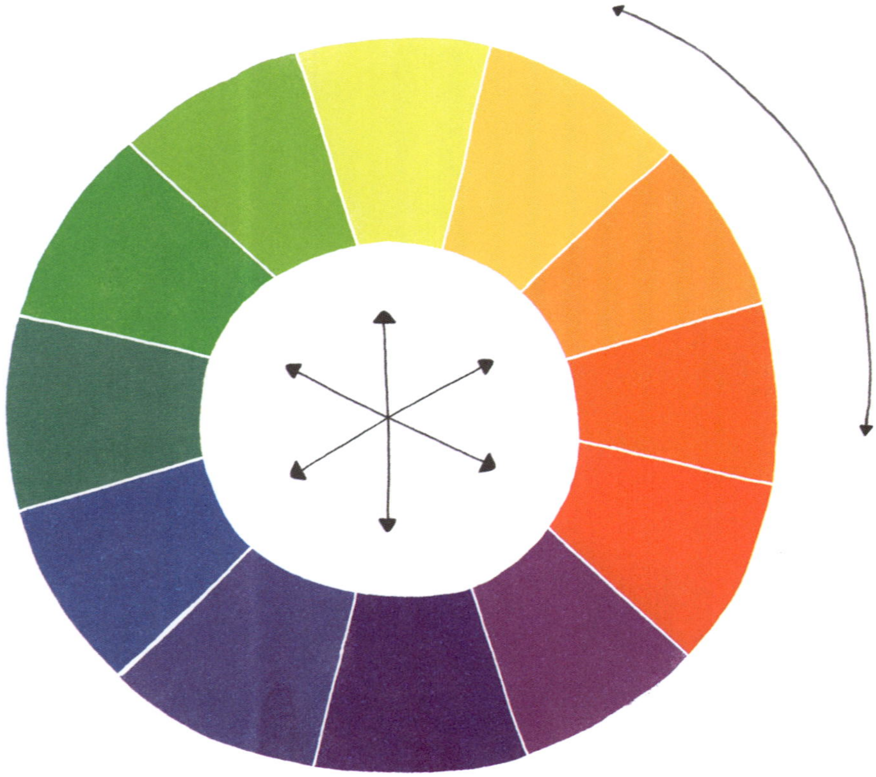

There are three **primary colors**: red, yellow, and blue. These colors cannot be created by mixing other colors. Mixing two primary colors produces a **secondary color**: orange, green, and purple. Mixing a primary color with a secondary color produces a **tertiary color**: red-orange, red-purple, yellow-orange, yellow-green, blue-green, and blue-purple. Red, orange, and yellow are "warm" colors; green, blue, and purple are "cool" colors.

Colors directly across from one another, like yellow and purple, blue and orange, and green and red are **complementary** (see arrows inside color wheel). Together, these colors will make your artwork bright and bold. Colors next to each other, such as yellow-orange and orange are **analogous** (see arrow on the outside of the color wheel). These colors look harmonious and pleasing to the eye.

COLOR & MOOD

Colors can inspire different feelings, emotions, and energy. They also are an effective way to influence the tone of your drawings. For example, gray is a great color choice for a too-cool cat, whereas orange and yellow might look better on a silly, mischievous cat. How might you use the colors below to communicate the mood of a drawing or doodle?

Bright & happy

Vibrant pastel

Chic & modern

Cool & calm

Drawing Cute Cats Step by Step

PERSIAN

1

Draw a fluffy oval for the body and triangular ears.

2

Add a cute face and a bushy tail.

Add hatch lines for a long fur coat. 3

Color it in!

SELKIRK REX

1

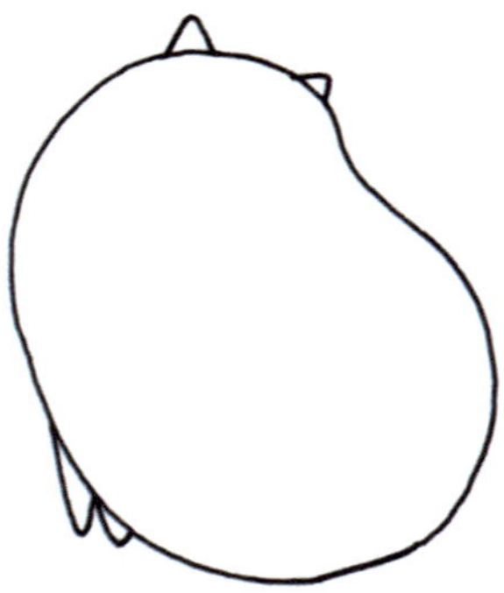

Outline a bean shape for the body. Add triangles for ears and legs.

2

Go over the outline with scalloped lines to create fluff.

3

Add a fluffy oval tail and cute face.

4

Add fluffy fur.

5

Add color!

JAPANESE BOBTAIL

1

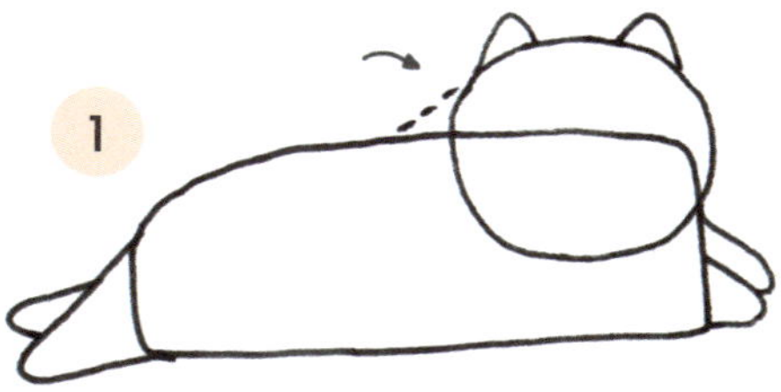

Use a circle and long rectangle to create the body. Then add triangles for ears and legs.

2

Trace the outline and erase any unused sketch lines.

3

Add a face and a fluffy circle tail.

Cute little round tail!

4

Add markings and color it in!

ABYSSINIAN

1

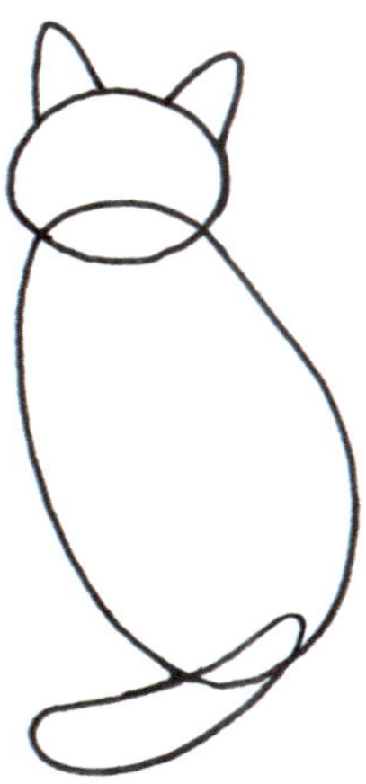

Draw a circle and oval for the body. Then add a curvy tail and triangular ears.

2

Trace the body outline and erase any sketch lines.

3

Add long legs, big almond-shaped eyes, nose, and whiskers.

Large, pointed ears!

4

Finish with color!

RAGDOLL

1

Draw a fluffy oval for the body. Add triangular ears and legs.

2

Draw big almond-shaped eyes, nose, and whiskers.

3

Add a bushy tail and a bow tie.

4

Add markings and color.

QUICK TIPS

Scribble two fluffy ovals together to create a body.

Use simple shapes to start your drawings each time. It's easy!

BRITISH SHORTHAIR

1

Draw an oval first; then draw a curvy tail. Add triangular ears.

2

Add a cute face.

3

Draw a bow tie.

4

Add color.

QUICK TIPS

Start with a bean-shaped body.

Try experimenting with different patterns to create different breeds.

Turn it into a Scottish Fold by changing the ears to folded ones.

Long live the British Shorthair: a hearty breed that can live into its late teens!

Cat Faces

Sneaky

Scared

Confident

Relaxed

Cheerful and Playful

Confused

Sleepy

Angry

Curious

Sleepy

Worried

Surprised

Cat Dragons

SLEEPY DRAGON

FLYING DRAGON

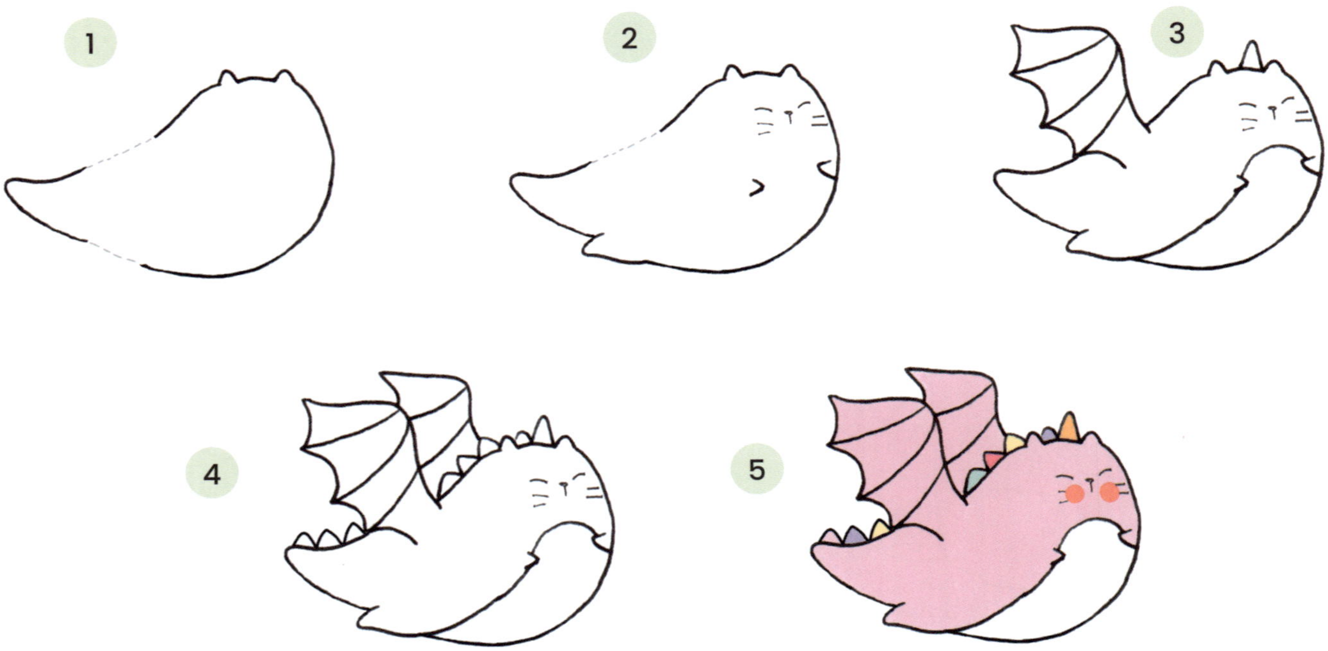

Out-of-This-World Cats

GHOST CAT

UNICORN CAT

ANGEL CAT

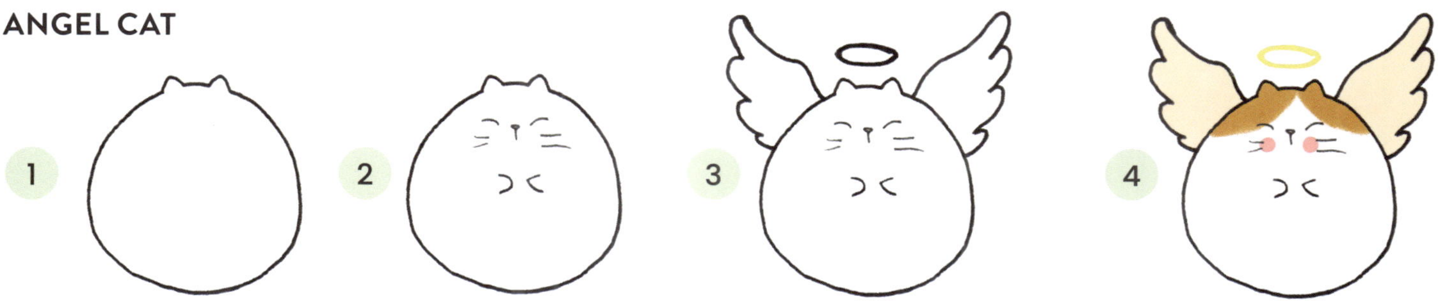

Star Sign Cats

WHAT'S YOUR SIGN?

ARIES
March 21 – April 19
Warm, lovable, honest

TAURUS
April 20 – May 20
Resilient and stubborn

GEMINI
May 21 – June 20
Communicative and charismatic

CANCER
June 21 – July 22
Outgoing and social

LEO
July 23 – August 22
Passionate and loyal

VIRGO
August 23 – September 22
Perfectionist and organized

LIBRA
September 23 – October 22
Balanced and people-pleasing

SCORPIO
October 23 – November 21
Mysterious and loyal

SAGITTARIUS
November 22 – December 21
Adventurous and frank

CAPRICORN
December 22 – January 19
Practical and determined

AQUARIUS
January 20 – February 18
Assertive and complex

PISCES
February 19 – March 20
Compassionate and creative

ARIES

1

2

3

4

TAURUS

1

2

3

4

5

6

CANCER

LEO

SAGITTARIUS

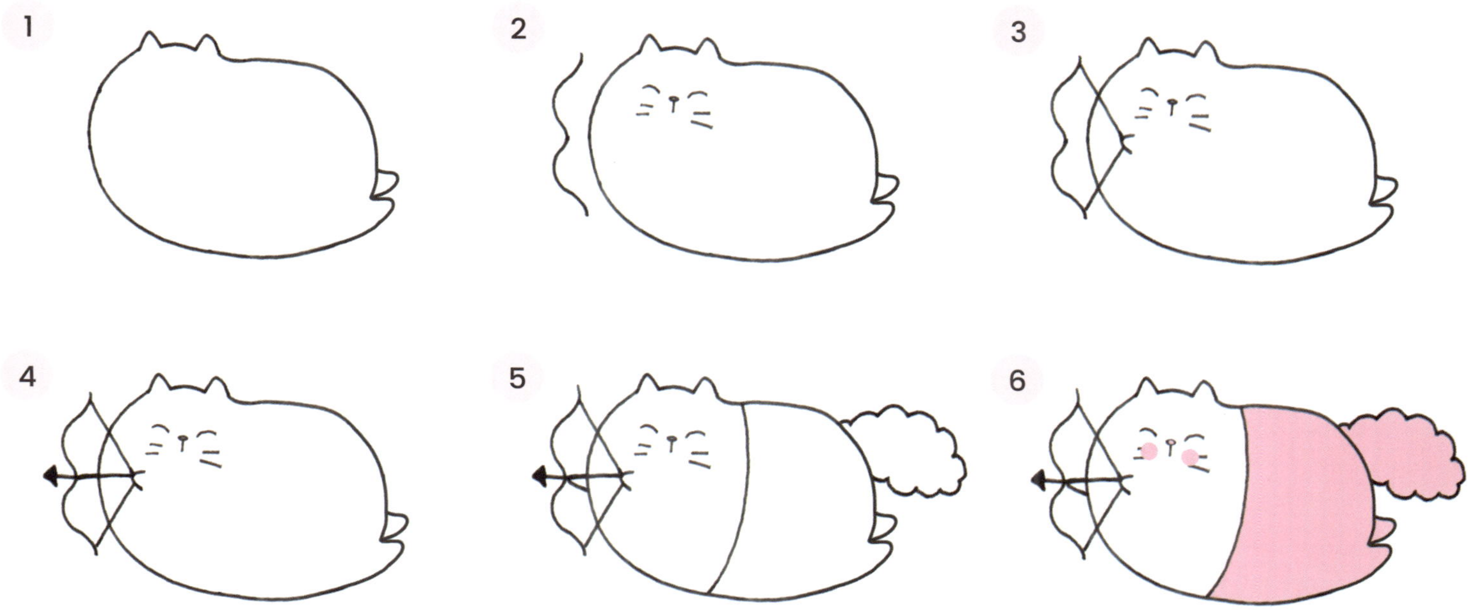

CAPRICORN

Beckoning Cat

MANEKI-NEKO

The Beckoning Cat, known as Maneki-neko in Japanese, is said to bring good luck to its owner. Traditionally, it's a calico Japanese Bobtail.

BOTH PAWS RAISED

To bring money, good fortune, and customers.

KOBAN COIN

Represents wealth that is brought to its owner.

BIB & BELL

The lucky cat is adorned with a bib and bell, the same way as it was dressed by its wealthy owner in the Edo period in Japan.

BECKONING CAT

1

2

3

4

5

6

Left Paw Raised
To invite people and customers

Carp
Symbolizes wealth

Right Paw Raised
To bring money and good fortune

Hammer
It's a money-mallet to summon wealth

Black
To ward off evil spirits and stalkers

Pink
To beckon love into your life

Gold
To bring wealth into your life

Green
To bring success to your studies

Clothes & Accessories

WARM MITTENS

FLUFFY SOCKS

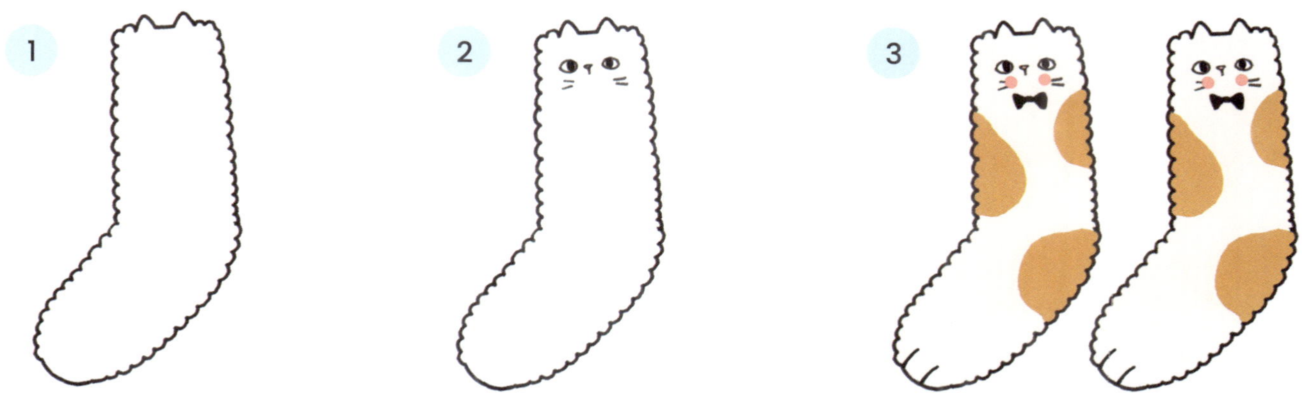

TOASTY BEANIE

EARMUFFS

KEYCHAIN

SUNGLASSES

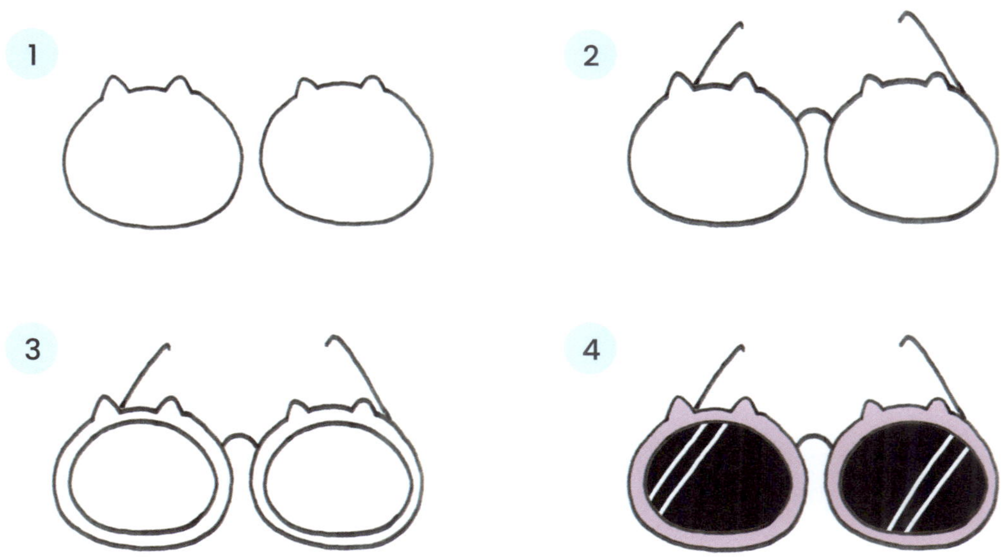

PLUSH SLIPPERS

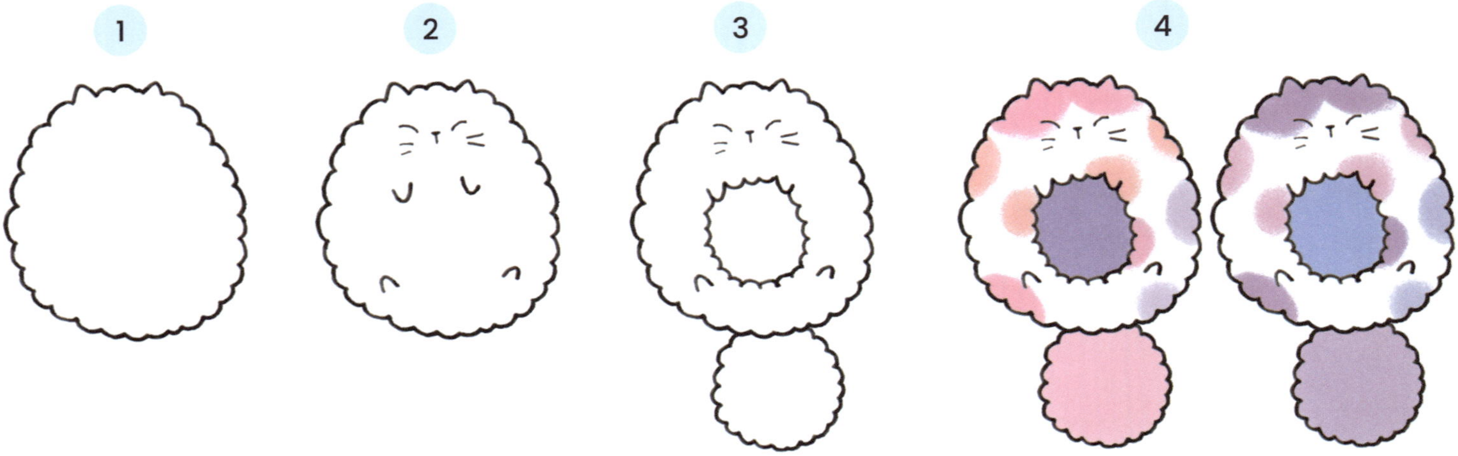

FLUFFY SANDALS

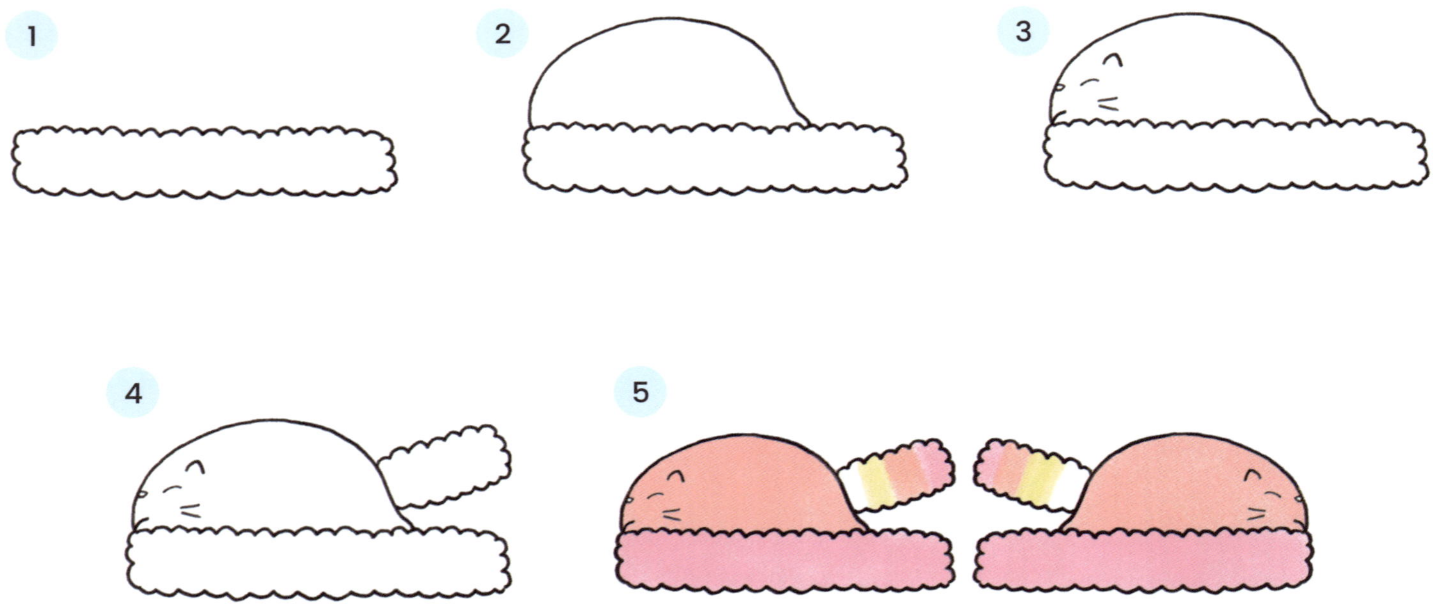

ANXIOUS CAT COIN PURSE

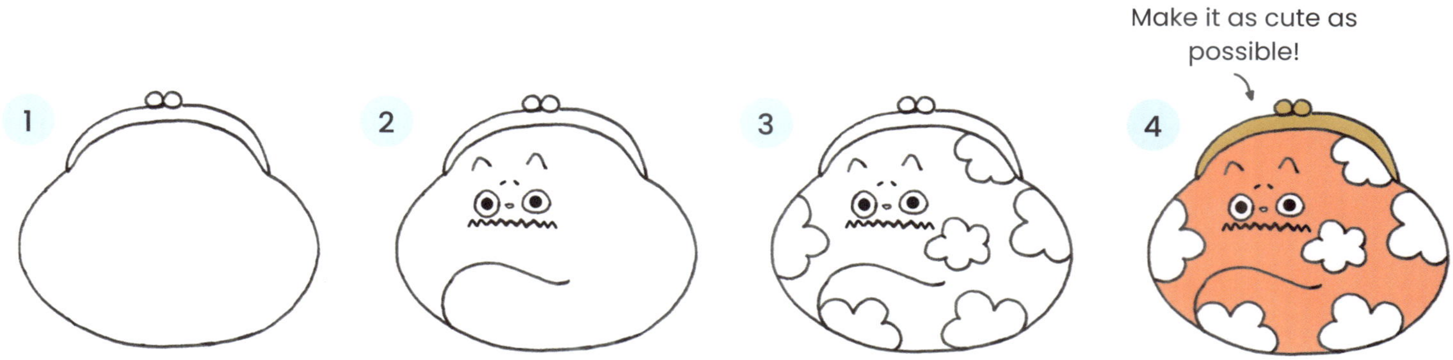

WORRIED BUCKET BAG

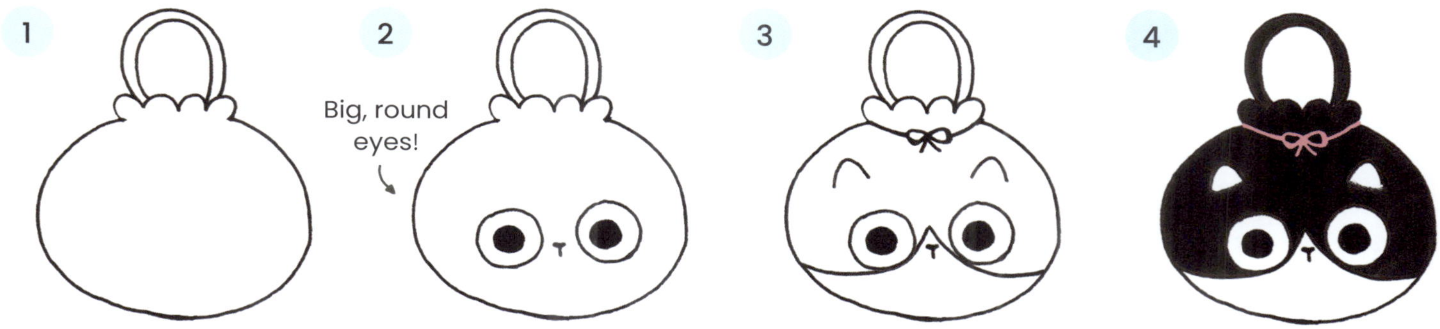

REGRETFUL BRIEFCASE

Cat Food

FELINE FRUITS & VEGGIES

Insecure Broccoli

Unsettled Avocado

Alarmed Cauliflower

Cautious Garlic

Petrified Cabbage

SCARED MUSHROOM

COOL COCONUT

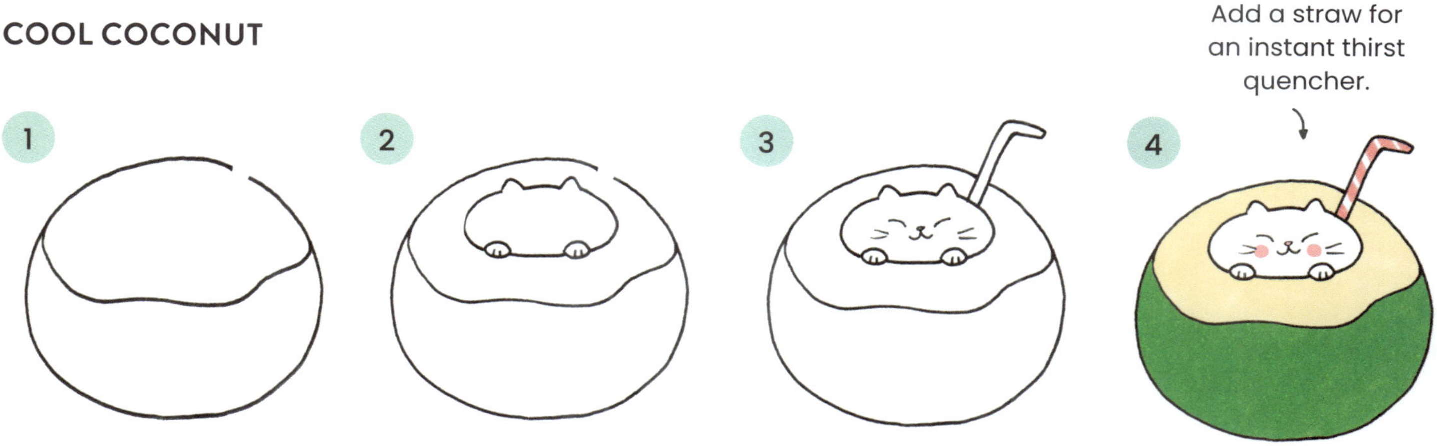

PURRFECT PEACH

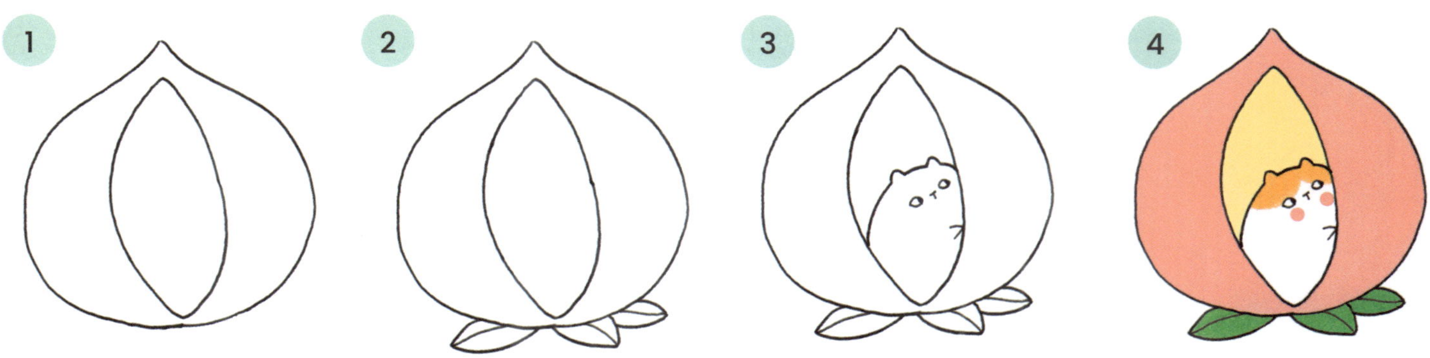

MATURE BANANA

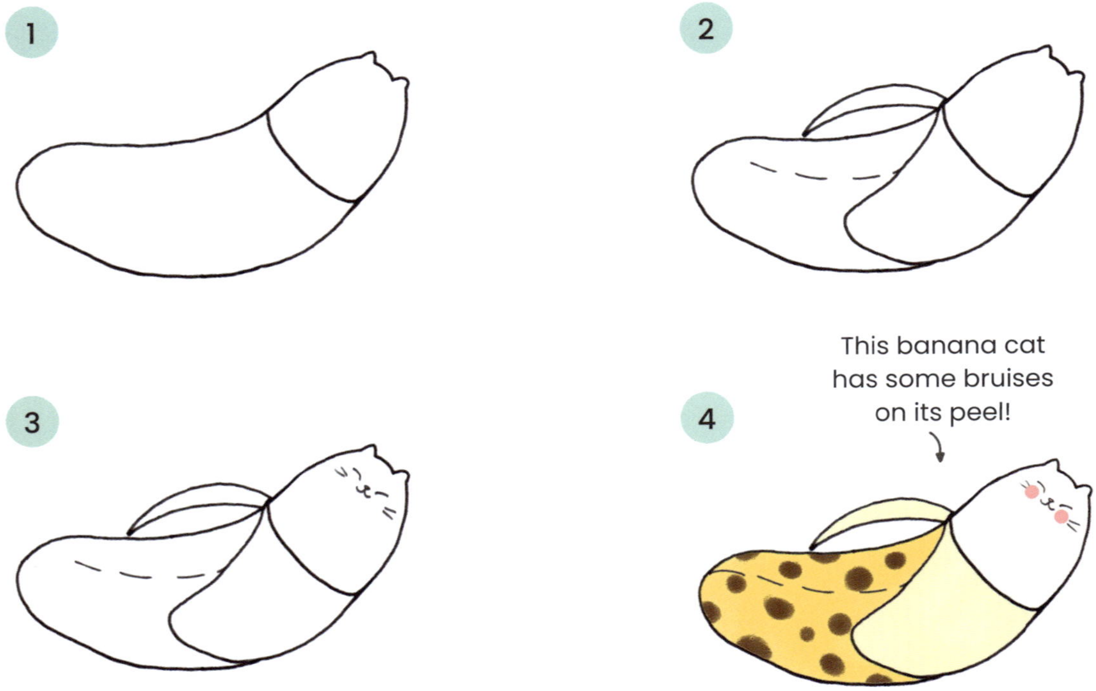

TANGERINE TABBY

KIWI KITTY

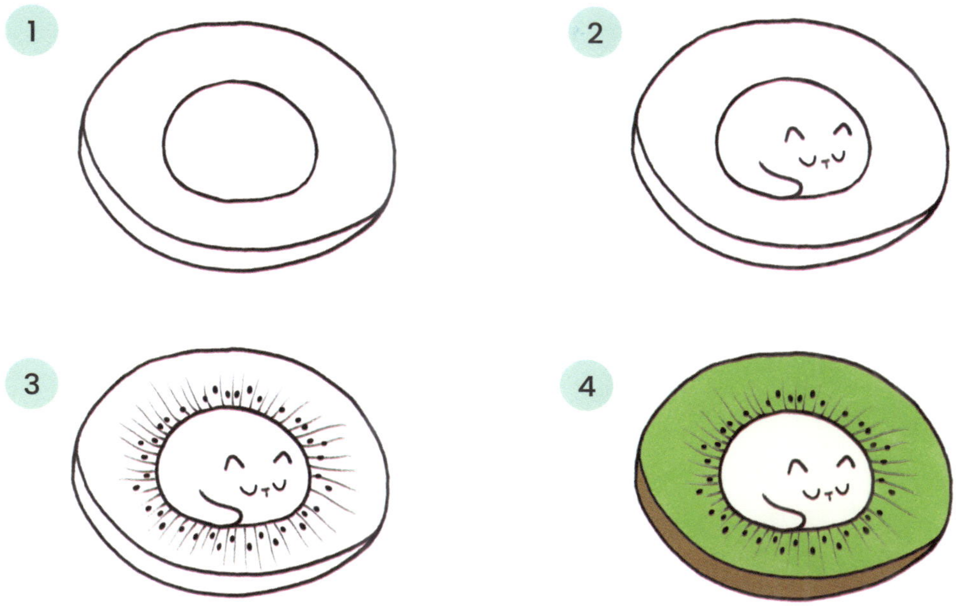

KING DURIAN KITTY CATS

The durian is a large fruit from Southeast Asia that has a strong smell and rich taste.

White loaf
Fine and simple

Muffin
Soft and buttery

Sourdough
Sour and airy

Bagel
Dense and chewy

Mochi bun
Elastic with a great depth of flavor

Cross bun
Cross and spicy with a hint of cinnamon

BIG LOAF

1

2

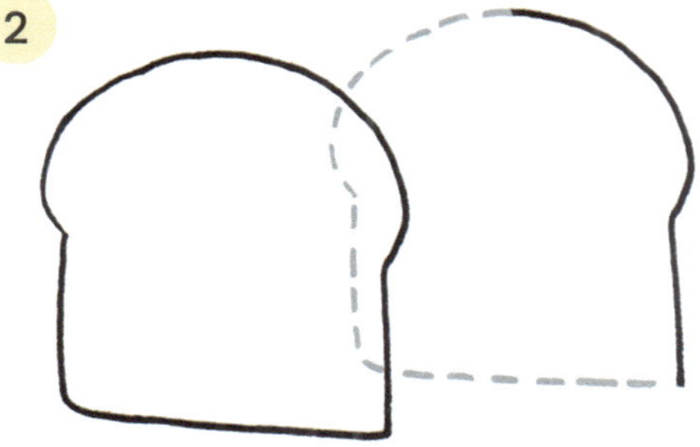

3

4

5

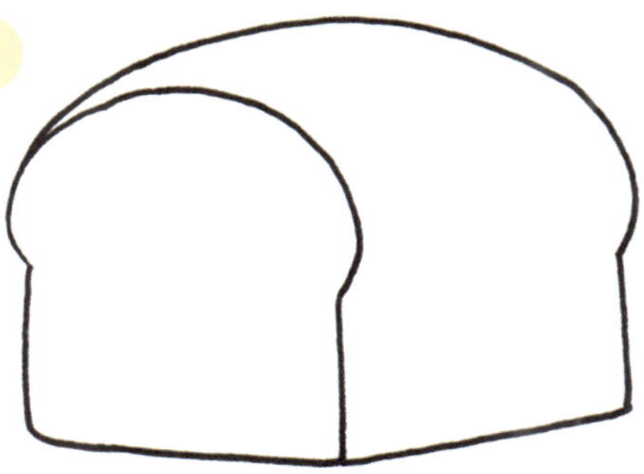

6

Self-conscious Penne

Loving Farfalle Couple
Also known as bow tie pasta

Spooky Spaghetti

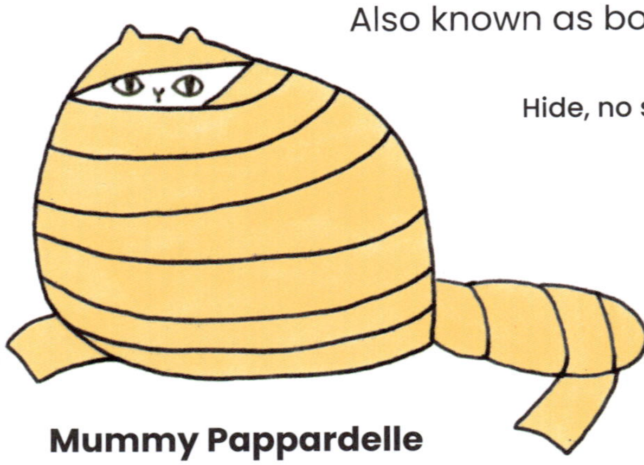

Mummy Pappardelle
Large, broad, and flat pasta

Alert Ditalini

Magical Elbow
Rainbow-shaped pasta

Conchigliette
Small seashell pasta

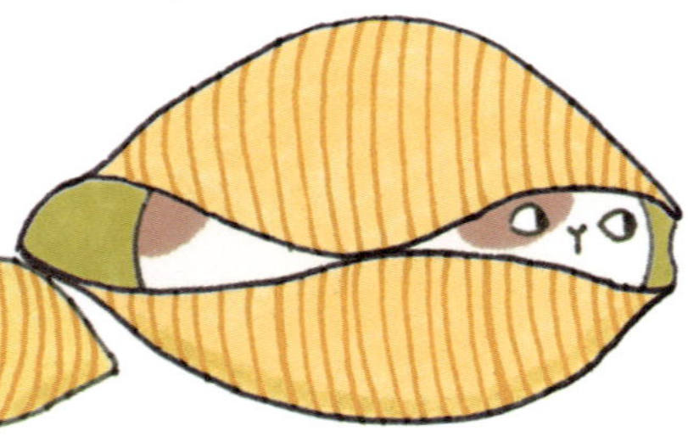

Shy Conchiglioni
Big seashell pasta

Encouraging Conchiglie
Medium seashell pasta

OVERJOYED POPCORN

SMILEY HOT DOG-CAT

COMFY BURGER

CLAUSTROPHOBIC TACO

RESTED PANCAKE

CHEERFUL INSTANT NOODLES

Sushi Cats

SLEEPY NIGIRI

1

2

3

4

FLOPPY SASHIMI

1

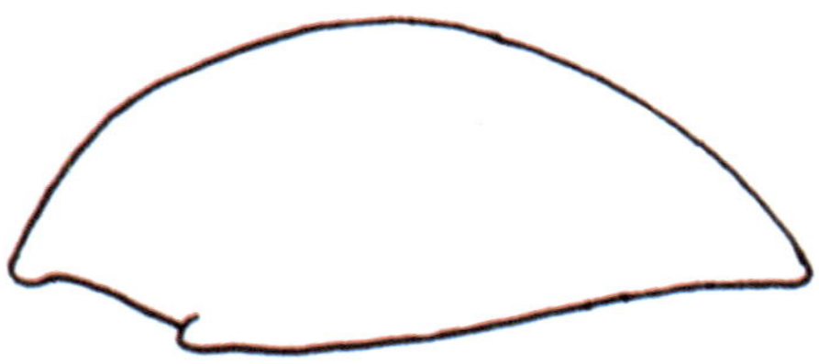

2

3

4

Sashimi is a slice of raw fish.

Tamago Sushi
A sushi made
with omelet.

Triangle Onigiri
A rice ball.

Rolled-up Maki
Maki is a rice
cylinder with
seaweed.

Prawn Tempura Maki
A battered and
deep-fried maki.

SECRET MENU

Meow Sushi

680 Calico Street
Cat Town

Maki in the Making

Hard-working Maki

Maki Set

Sleepy Nigiri

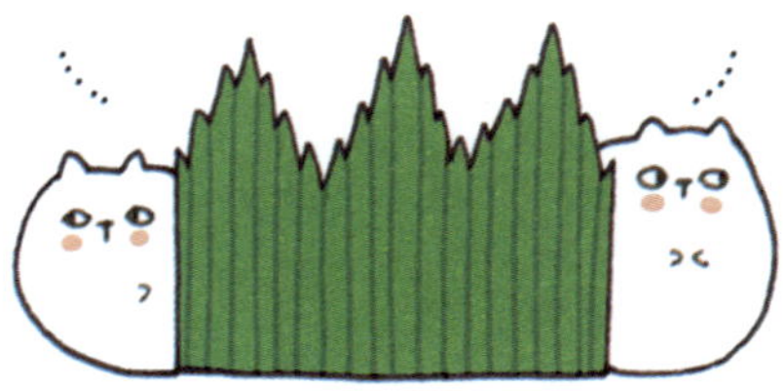
Currently Unavailable

Tamago Sushi

Chef's Special Onigiri

Uncut Gem Maki

Twitchy Tamago Sushi

Mer-cat Nigiri

Cuddly Onigiri

Café au Cat

GINGER TABBY LATTE

Tabby Mocha

Moggy Matcha Latte

Calico Bubble Tea

Sweets Shoppe

MACARONS

Rose

Lavender

Lemon

Vanilla and Caramel

Trio
Lemon, peach, and coffee

LICORICE & STRAWBERRY MACARON

SOPHISTICATED GATO GELATO

VANILLA ICE CREAM CATWICH

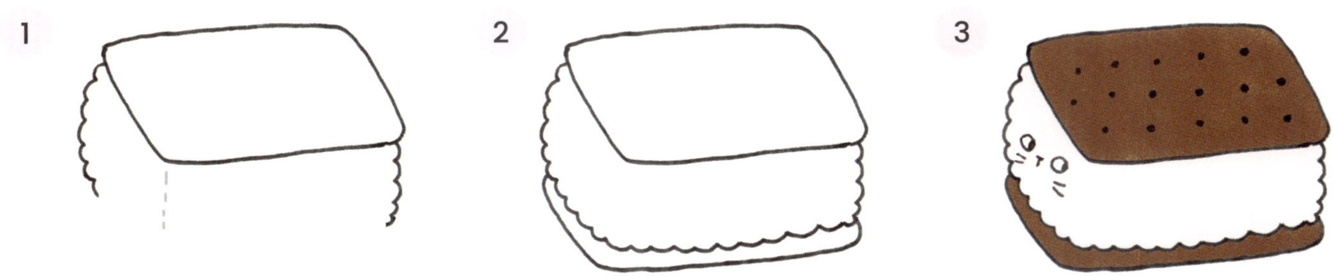

TANGLED ICE LOLLY

MELTING DOUBLE STICK

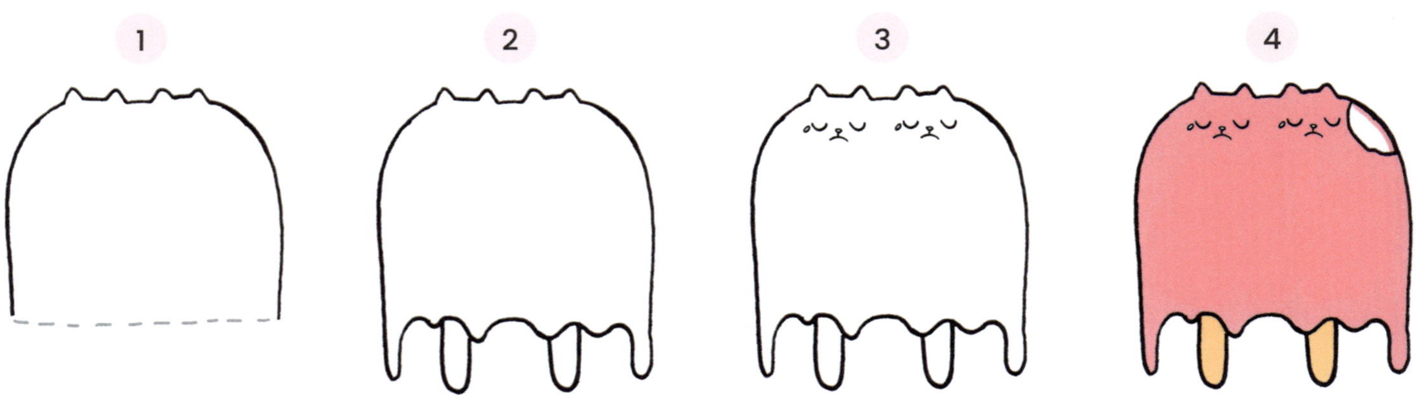

Soufflé
Delicate and light

Swiss roll
Dizzy and delicious rolled sponge cake with jam

Éclair
Glossy and silky

Muffin
Filling and portable

CAT CAKE DONUTS

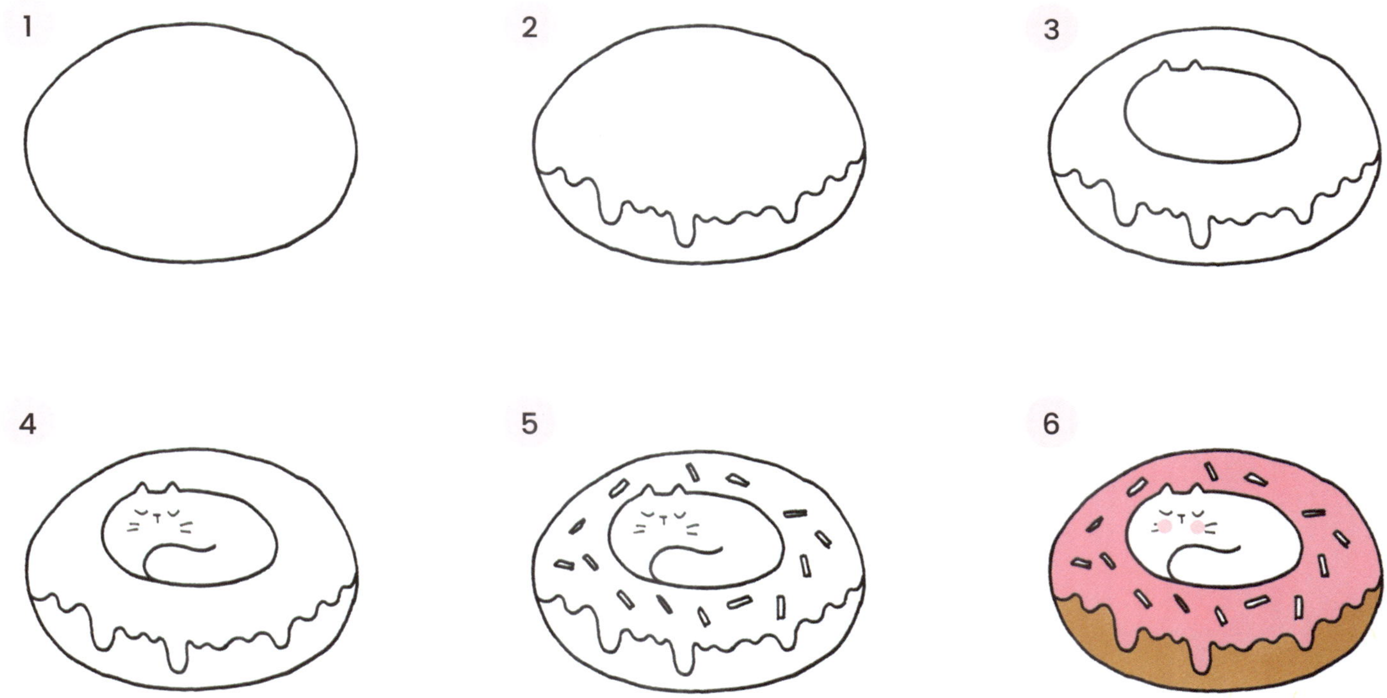

Cat Lady's Crockery

TEAPOT

MUG

Cactus Cats

Bishop's cat
Reflect on the things you are grateful for.

Prickly pear
Do yoga.

Moon cactus
Sit in the sunlight.

Chin cactus
Practice mindfulness.

Barrel cactus
Breathe in, breathe out. Meditate.

Bunny ear cactus
Eat nutritious food.

BUNNY EAR

1

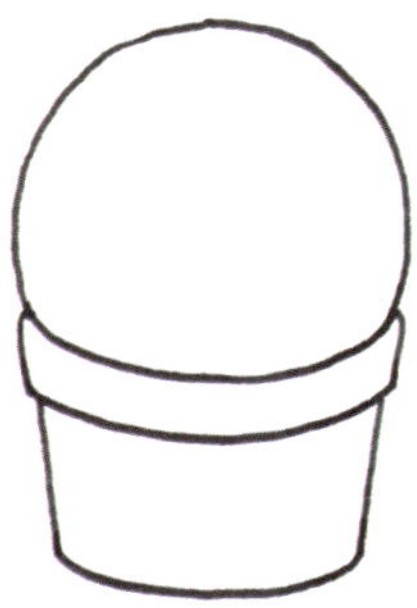

2

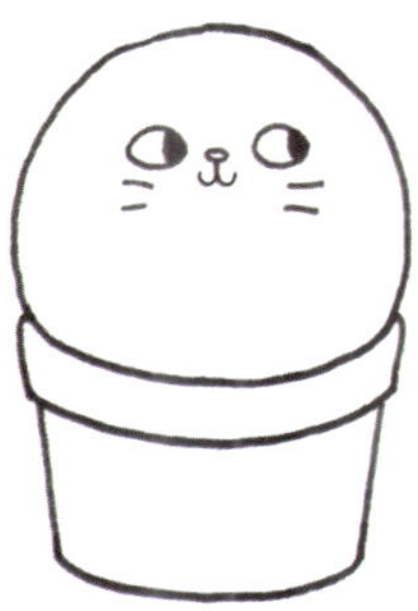

3

4

Cats at Home

BOOKSHELF

DESK LAMP

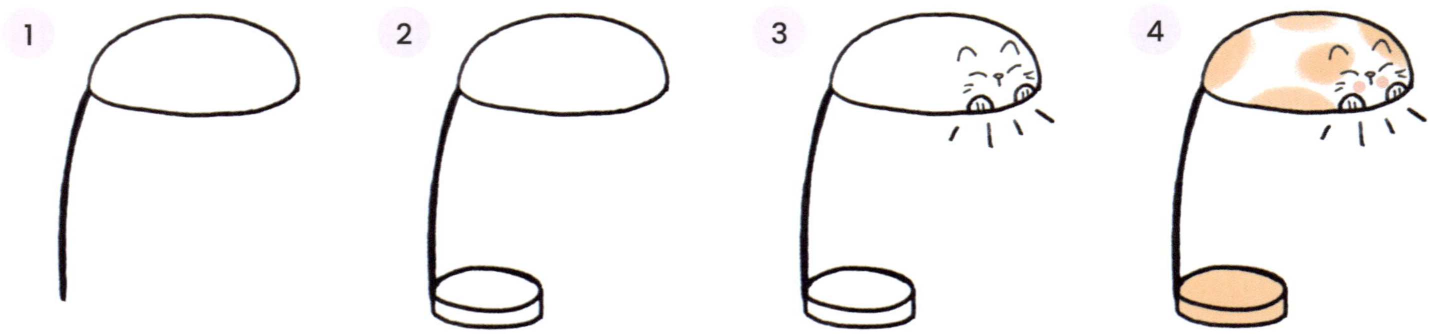

CHAISE LOUNGE

Armchair

Chair inspired by Arne Jacobsen

Stool

Sofa

TOASTER

MIXER

OLD-SCHOOL TELEPHONE

TEA KETTLE

Stationery Cats

PENCIL CASE

PENCIL SHARPENER

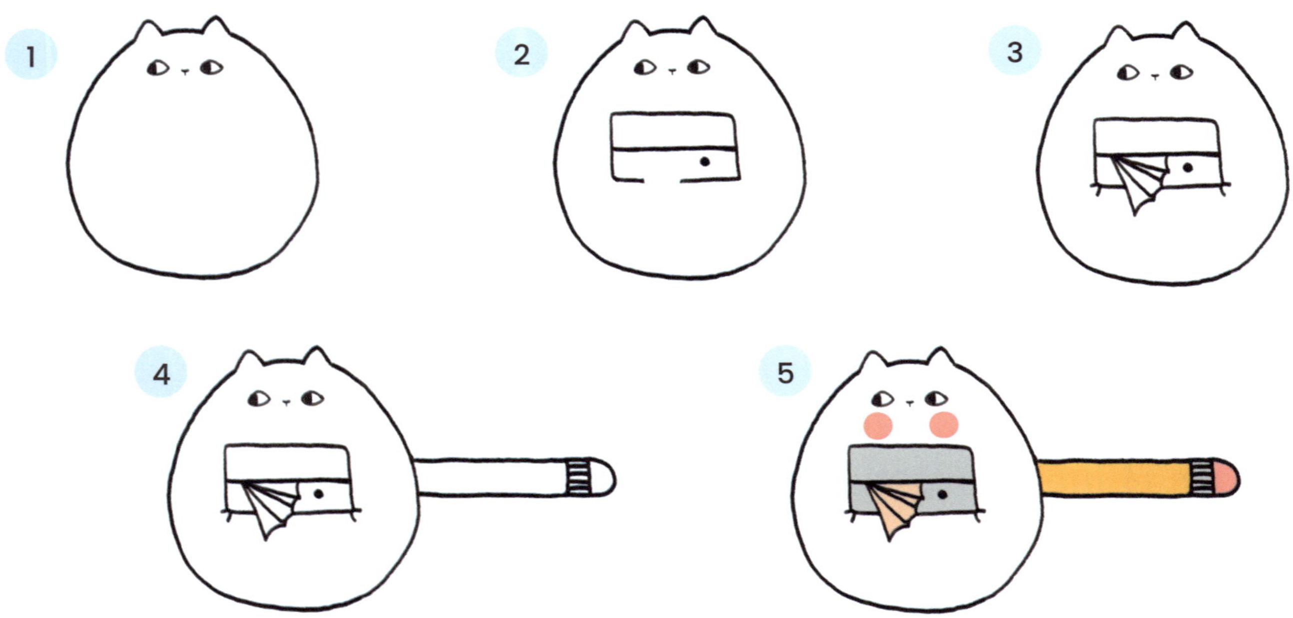

MECHANICAL PENCIL

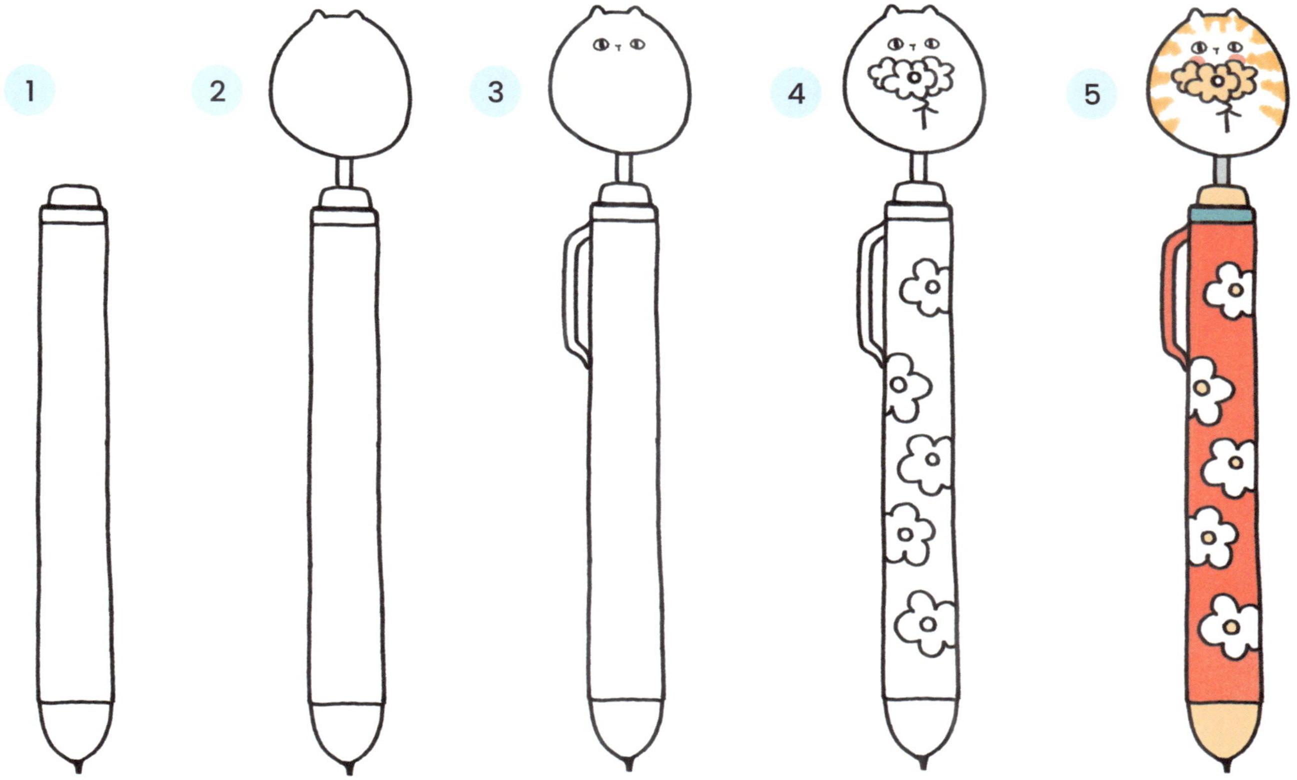

JOURNAL

BINDER CLIP

STAPLER

ERASER

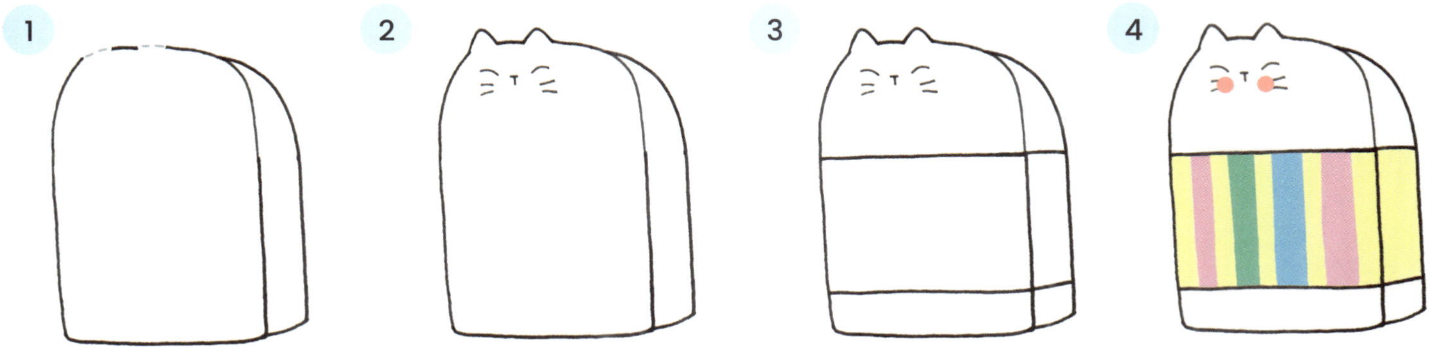

PENCIL

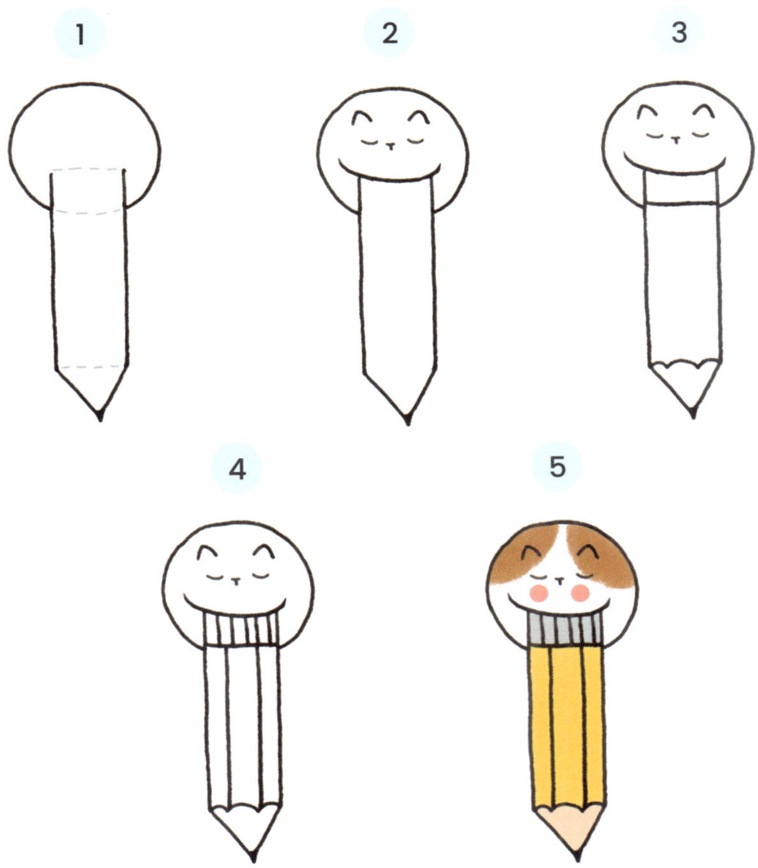

Colored pencil

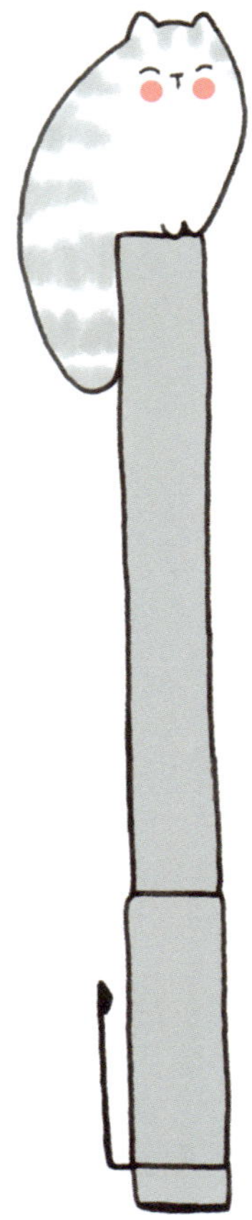

Liner pen

Holiday Cats

CHRISTMAS STOCKING

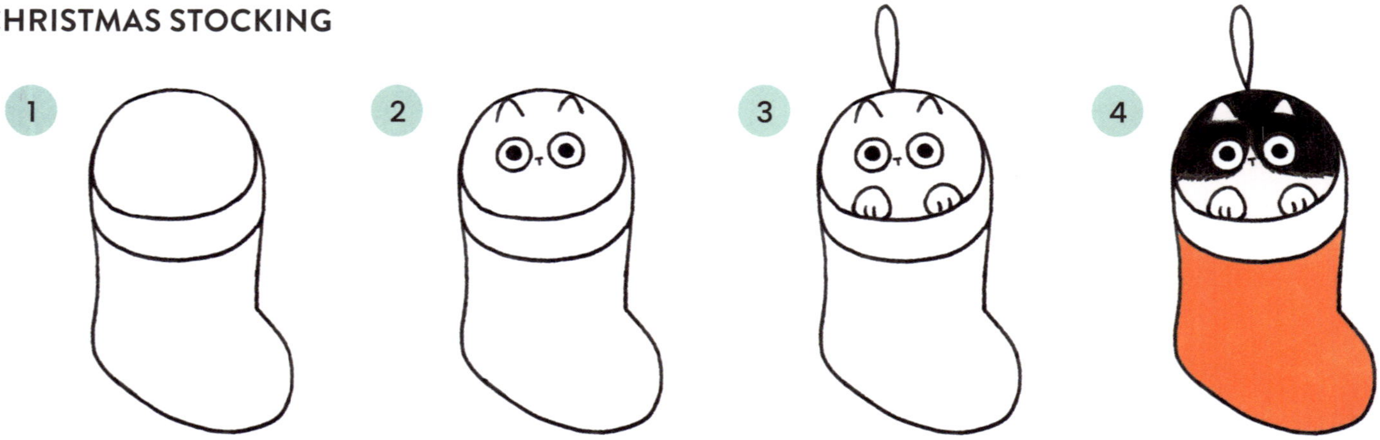

CHRISTMAS LIGHTS

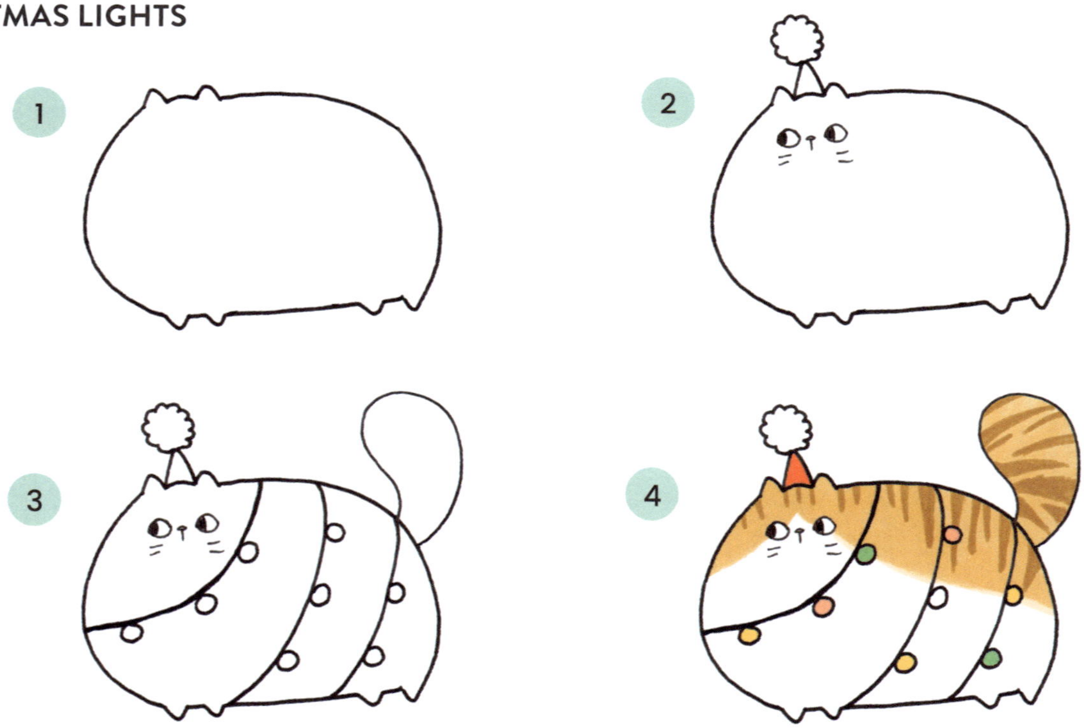

Merry Cat-mas!

CHRISTMAS TREE

HALLOWEEN VAMPIRE BAT CAT

MUMMY CAT

PUMPKIN CAT

1

2

3

4

5

6

Artistic Cats

PIET MONDRIAN

Piet Mondrian is best known for his abstract geometric-inspired paintings. He developed a simplified style by restricting his palette to the three primary colors—blue, yellow, and red—on a grid of black vertical and horizontal lines on a white background. If he were to have drawn a cat, it probably would have looked something like this!

YAYOI KUSAMA

You can tell Yayoi Kusama's obsession with polka dots when you see her artworks. It's her most recognizable motif. Pumpkins are another trademark of her works; she started drawing them when she was a kid. This is my cat portrait inspired by Yayoi Kusama.

About the Author

Lulu Mayo is passionately committed to daydreaming in the fantasy art world where cats and mysterious creatures live. Cats have always been at the center of her works, and you will find them in each of the 20 books she has published worldwide, which have been translated and sold into more than 20 different territories. Follow Lulu on Instagram: @lulu_mayo_art or visit lulumayo.com.